A Cat Called Tess

Russell Turner

Bassman Books

For Mum, who never gets thanked enough

Published by Bassman Books, Burnside Cottage, Newhall, Balblair, Dingwall, IV7 8LT

First published in 2012

Copyright © Russell Turner 2012

The author asserts his moral right under the Copyright, Designs
and Patents Act 1988 to be identified as the author of this work

A catalogue record for this book is available from the British Library

ISBN 978-0-9567908-2-8

Printed by Big Sky, The Press Building, 305 The Park, Findhorn, Forres, IV36 3TE

Layout and design by Russell Turner

To buy any of the photographs visit www.russellturner.org

This
is
Tess

Tess lives in
a cottage in
the Highlands
of Scotland.

She likes to
explore the
countryside...

...Climb on the walls around the farm next door...

...And hide in the woods.

When Tess
is thirsty she
has a drink...

...Then goes
to play in
the old farm
buildings...

...And one of
the hollow logs
piled up
outside them...

...But she likes her garden too.

Tess has
lots of trees
to climb...

...Although

some are

very tall...

...With branches where she can rest.

There are
places
for a nap...

...Places
to hide...

...And a very comfortable upside-down flowerpot!

Inside her cottage, Tess likes to watch the birds...

...But what she likes best of all is to sleep...

...Especially on her warm shelf above the radiator.

Tess is
a very
happy cat.